Thomas's Joke Book

Also by Sarah Kennedy

Thomas's Joke Book

Compiled by
Sarah Kennedy

Michael O'Mara Humour

First published in Great Britain in 2004 by
Michael O'Mara Books Limited
9 Lion Yard
Tremadoc Road
London SW4 7NQ

A CIP catalogue record for this book is available from the British Library

ISBN 1-84317-117-1

1 3 5 7 9 10 8 6 4 2

Designed and typeset by www.envydesign.co.uk

Printed and bound in England by Cox & Wyman Ltd, Reading, Berks

A royalty of 5% of the retail price of this book on every copy sold
will go to the NSPCC.

FOREWORD

Firstly, I do hope you enjoy *Thomas's Joke Book*. I know I'm biased but believe me, whether you are aged four to eighty-four, there is something here for everyone. Our weekday programmes on Radio 2 between 6 and 7.30 a.m. illustrate the unique British sense of humour. I never quite know which topic our listeners will go with. Recently we've had vicars getting locked in loos (in Venice of all places), which started a stream of 'Got Caught Short' stories. Excuse the pun. Tins found in cupboards dated 1949? We had a tin of guavas in syrup found in Granny's pantry dated 1941. Then there's been the saga of the pets that steal, nicking food and dragging the neighbour's hot, beautifully cooked roast lamb through the cat flap. 'What happened to the Sunday roast?' wailed Doris. Better keep schtum, methinks, eh?

And there are more bizarre stories . . . Two listeners, holidaying in Spain: wife goes to the loo before bed and finds a fully grown eagle perched on the loo-roll holder, flapping its wings! Early next morning he was still there, but in the bath this time. Husband stark naked, armed only with a bath towel, effected a 'release into the wild'. Result? A very angry eagle, still flapping and squawking, flies to the nearest tree and glares at the couple the entire day!

As you can see, the *Dawn Patrol* taps into a rich seam of human and real life.

Thomas, the inspiration for this fun book, lives with his family in the adjoining village. You can read about my gaffe on the back of the book! I had to put things right. Well, I wasn't to know his sainted mother – another Sarah – had decided her boys were watching too much breakfast TV, and she would wean them on to Radio 2. She switched on to hear me tell Thomas's joke:

Q: How did the chewing gum cross the road?
A: On the bottom of the chicken's foot.

The rest is history!

Niki Catlow has done some super-fab cartoons, as have the 28th Silver Jubilee Cubs and 20th A Island Brownie Pack, so thank you to all parties! Thomas was a natural star at the photoshoot for the cover. Young Birman, one of our five cats, decided he'd get in on the picture. He's a terrible thief. I once heard a plastic bag rustling in the dining room and he had half-inched the meat for the weekend. All you could see was the moving bag being pushed round the carpet and a swishing chocolatey tail. He emerged triumphant with the string of sausages! I beat him to it and rescued the bacon with a rugby tackle.

Do enjoy the jokes, and I've slotted in some Terrible Twos for no extra charge! It's been grand working again with my Much Beloved who took the photos, and with editor May Corfield. She has two children and as she laughed till she had tears running down her cheeks, I am quietly confident we are on to a winner!

Here's to Thomas.

SARAH KENNEDY, AUGUST 2004

Q: Nana, how does a bee get to work?

I don't know, Jack. How does a
bee get to work?

A: On the buzz.

Jack Monkman (age three)

Q: What's black and shouts 'Knickers!'

A: Crude oil.

Cherry Roomes and Susan Martin

Why did the Zebra have stripes?
Because it didn't like   Spots

by Kathleen Chan

My two-year-old granddaughter Evie recently embarked on some baking with my wife Sue, and as many toddlers do, she insisted on eating the uncooked mixture. Generally, Sue didn't mind, but as Evie had recently been ill, her grandma felt it necessary to keep a tight rein on such activity. 'Evie, don't eat the mixture – wait until the buns are baked,' rebuked Grandma. Evie apologized.

Thirty seconds later, Grandma issued another reminder: 'Evie, I said don't eat the mixture – the buns won't take long.'

'Sorry, Grandma,' came the reply.

Fifteen seconds later, Grandma found it necessary to have words again: 'Evie, what have I just said?'

To which Evie gasped and curtly replied: 'Grandma, I am NOT eating it – I'm just wiping my fingers with my mouth!' Needless to say, Grandma was speechless.

David and Sue Maris, and Evie Alice Ward

Q: What do you get if you give a cat a lemon?

A: A sour puss.

Bernard Tate

Q: Which painter always had a cold?

A: Titian.

James Robinson

Q: What's white, green and white, and jumps?

A: A frog sandwich.

Janie Drury

Did you hear about the two men who stole a calendar?

They got six months each.

Ian D. Mullen

3

When our grandson Alex, who is now six, was at playschool he mentioned to his mum that he'd been told off by a teacher. When asked what he'd done, he replied, 'Some of the children were being naughty and I accidentally joined in.'

George Hill

Q: What sort of false teeth can you buy for a dollar?

A: Buck teeth.

Pat Mason

Q: There are two cats, one English and one French, who have a race across the English Channel. The English cat is called One, Two, Three and the French cat is called Un, Deux, Trois.
Which cat won the race?

A: The English cat, because Un, Deux, Trois cat sank.

Freya Davis (age nine)

Q: Why did the turtle cross the road?

A: It was the chicken's day off.

Claire Chin (age seven)

Q: What did one flea say to the other?

A: Shall we walk or take the dog?

Sarah Ladbrook

When our younger daughter was about five years old, she was engrossed in a documentary about bees, which focused on the queen, drones and workers that all lived together in the hive. She still seemed to be rather preoccupied with the subject over tea, before eventually coming to the following conclusion: 'Daddy, you have served your purpose!'

Andy from Sheffield

Q: What is an Egyptian king's favourite chocolate?

A: Pharaoh Rocher.

Ben Gondolo (age eight)

Q: How do you make toast in the jungle?

A: Under a gorilla.

Roger Jakeman

Q: What do you call a smelly fairy?

A: Stinkerbell.

Carys Fisser and Helen Campbell

If my father is Icelandic and my mother is Cuban, does this make me an Ice Cube?

Ian Fuller

Q: What do you call a carpet fitter?

A: Walter Wall.

Gordon Evans

Q: What's green and furry, and goes up and down?

A: A gooseberry in a lift.

Mags Lacy and Amanda Coates

Many years ago we had a trip to a snowy Munich with our four boys. We were sitting at breakfast in a lovely pension with people entering the dining room and saying quietly, 'Morgen, morgen.' Eventually Ashley, our youngest son, who was then about four, firmly and deliberately put down his knife and fork at the side of his plate and said, 'How does everybody know our name?'

Frank Morgan

Q: What do you call two Spanish firemen?

A: Hose A and Hose B.

Anthony Watson

When our daughter Aneira was four, she was very keen on serving meals made up of plastic food. My mother and I were sitting in the garden having one of Aneira's teas, when she asked, 'Grandma, would you like an orangutan?' Rather perplexed at what this culinary delight could be, Grandma accepted with interest, and was very amused to receive a meringue!

Karen Harrild

Apparently, one in five people in the world is Chinese, and there are five people in my family, so it must be one of them. It's either my mum or my dad, or my older brother Colin, or my younger brother Ho-Cha-Chu . . . but I think it's Colin.

Nick Benson

Two aerials meet on a roof, fall in love and get married.

The ceremony was rubbish, but the reception was brilliant.

Nick Benson

Q: What do policemen have in their sandwiches?

A: Truncheon meat.

Steve Gibbons

Rosie, our four-year-old, recently took me into her confidence and said, 'Dad, I know what those red flowers coming up in the garden are called, 'cos Mummy told me.'

'What's that, then?' I asked.

'Lipsyls,' she announced. So that is what tulips are now called in our house.

J. and C. Prowse

Q: What do you call a man with three wooden heads?

A: Edward Woodward.

James Robinson

Q: Why did Eve move to New York?

A: She fell for a big apple.

Bernard Tate

Q: What do you get from whisky-drinking chickens?

A: Scotch eggs.

Ian Fuller

Q: How do you stop rabbits digging holes in your garden?

A: Lock up your tool shed.

Mike Bedrock

Q: Why did the orange go to the doctor?
A: Because it wasn't peeling well!

BY: Harleen Grewal 6A Age:10

When my daughter Wren was about four, I picked her up from school one day and asked her what she had learned during her lessons. She said they had talked about things that were 'above and below'. So when I asked her what was above us, she replied that it was sky, clouds and birds. Then I asked what was below, expecting to hear things like tunnels and caves, but she confidently replied, 'Hell.'

Len Eccles

A tiny tot was saying his prayers at night, and his mother was listening as he knelt beside his bed. As the little lad was whispering quietly, his mother said, 'I can't hear you, dear,' to which the boy replied, 'I'm not talking to you!'

Mac from Stockport

Q: What do you call two rows of cabbages?

A: A dual cabbageway.

Sandy and Pete Bromley

Q: What do you get if you cross a chicken with a cement mixer?

A: A bricklayer.

Richard Mayston

Q: What do you call a fast-food snack served at a church fête?

A: A hymn burger.

Helen Green

When my son was little, he loved asparagus soup, but he struggled to say the words. Once in a supermarket he shouted, 'Can we have some sparrow guts soup?' and to this day we always refer to it as that.

Jayne Freeman

Q: Where are the Andes?
A: On the end of your wristies.

Mags Lacy

'Mummy, does God use our bathroom?'

'No, why do you ask?'

'Because every morning Daddy bangs on the door and shouts, "Oh God, are you still in there?"'

Richard Mayston

A little girl was talking to her teacher about whales. The teacher said it was physically impossible for a whale to swallow a human being, because even though the whale is a very large mammal, its throat is very small. The little girl then raised the point that Jonah was swallowed by a whale. Irritated, the teacher reiterated that a whale could not swallow a human, as it was physically impossible. The little girl then said, 'When I get to heaven I'll ask Jonah.'
'What if Jonah went to Hell?' asked the teacher loftily.
The little girl replied,
'Then you can ask him!'

Douglas Adkins

Q: What do you put on a sore pig?

A: Oinkment.

Sue Edwards

Q: How do you start a pudding race?

A: Sago.

Di Kettle

Q: Why did the hedgehog cross the road?

A: To see his flatmate.

Jasmin Sharp

One day, when my son Ben was in the early stages of learning how to read (at a time when he was also a fussy eater), we were browsing through the window of the butcher's shop when I spotted him spelling out with his lips 'L, O, I, N chops'. 'Lion chops?' he asked excitedly. When we asked if he'd like some, he gave a very definite 'Yes!' We have eaten lion chops ever since in our house. Several years later, Ben is now a fire officer.

Eve Harris

Q: What do you call a camel with three humps?

A: Humphrey.

Baz from Wiltshire

Q: What are purple, and scream in fruit bowls?

A: Damsons in distress.

Mark from Reading

Q: What do you call a man with a spade in his head?

A: Doug.

Zoë Fitzgerald-Pool

Q: What did the ocean say to the other ocean?

A: Nothing, they just waved.

Mike Hesp

When my daughter Laura was five years old, she was allowed to greet guests at her father's birthday party before she left to spend the night with a friend. One guest asked, 'How old is Daddy today then?'

'Forty,' she replied.

The guests in mock horror put fingers to lips and in unison all said 'Shush!'

Laura looked a little bemused and then decided to put them at their ease. 'It's all right,' she whispered. 'He knows.'

Gill Balaguer

Three tortoises, Mick, Alan and Les,
decided to go on a picnic, so Mick packed
the picnic basket with beer and
sandwiches. Unfortunately, the picnic site
was ten miles away, so it took them ten
days to get there. When they arrived,
Mick unpacked the food and beer,
and said to Les,
'OK, give me the bottle opener.'
'I didn't bring it,' said Les.
'I thought you'd packed it.'
It turned out that no one had remembered
to pack the valuable item, and so they
were stuck ten miles from home without a
bottle opener. Mick and Alan begged Les to
go back for it, but he refused as he was
certain that the other two would eat all
the sandwiches. Following two hours of
persuasive arguments, and after Mick and
Alan had sworn on their tortoise lives that
they wouldn't eat the sandwiches,
Les finally agreed, and set off

down the road at a steady pace.
Twenty days passed by and he still hadn't
come back. Mick and Alan were starving,
but a promise was a promise, and they
didn't touch the sandwiches.

Another five days went by, and Les still
hadn't returned, but still they refused to
eat the sandwiches. Finally, they couldn't
take it any longer, so they each took out a
sandwich and, just as they were
about to take a bite, Les popped up from
behind a rock and shouted,
'I knew it . . . I'm not going!'

Pat Jackson

My grandson Sam often makes us laugh. When
he was three I asked him what his address was.
He replied that he didn't have a dress – he didn't
even have a skirt.

He is now four and this week, after his sister
Jessica had been to Brownies, I asked him if he
was going to go to Cubs when he was bigger. He
looked at me strangely, and said, 'Nanny, I'm
not old enough to go to pubs!'

Ann Eldridge

'I don't want to go to school today, Mummy. The teachers all think I'm an idiot, and the kids all hate me.'
'But you have to go, darling. You're the headmaster.'

Zoë Parrish (age five)

Q: What's the difference between a soldier and a sailor?

A: You can't dip your sailor in an egg.

Hannah Metesi (age four) and Rebecca Anderson

I collected my great-nephew after his first day at school. On meeting him at the gate, I asked him if he liked the school.

'Yes,' he replied. 'There's another James in my class, but he's got a different face to mine.'

Wendy Bozier

My friend drowned in a bowl of muesli. He was pulled in by a strong currant.

Brian Palmer

Q: What do you get if you cross a monkey with a flower?

A: A chimpansy.

Nancy Lavender

Q: What do cows like to do on a Saturday night?

A: Go to the mooooovies.

Sam Edgeley (age four)

'Knock, knock.'

'Who's there?'

'Lydia.'

'Lydia who?'

'Lydia teapot.'

Maggie Wells

My grand-nephew Brian was talking to his grandma, my sister-in-law. 'Grandma, what age are you?' he asked. As Grandma was slow or unwilling to reply, he asked again, 'Grandma, what age are you?' Still no reply so, in an exasperated tone, he said, 'Grandma, if you don't know how old you are, look in your pants. My underpants say "Age 5–6", and I'm five!'

Chris McAllister

Q: Why did the duck take the mirror back to the shop?

A: Because there was a quack in it.

Anna Ellerbeck (age three)

Q: What do you call a miserable pudding?

A: Apple grumble.

Pam Morton

There was once a man called 'Mind your own business' who had a dog called 'Trouble'. One day he lost his dog, and so he went to the police station to report it missing. The police officer on the front desk asked the man his name. He replied, 'Mind your own business.'

The policeman was angered by the man's apparent rudeness, and demanded, 'Are you looking for trouble?'

'Yes, how did you know?' replied the man.

Nick Hills

I have two nephews of five and three, both of whom are adorable. On a Sunday recently, their grandparents visited for the day. When they were all sitting down to lunch, the boys were quietly absorbing the dialogue between their elders as the various condiments were passed around the table. Suddenly, the younger boy chirped up, 'Can I have some of that horse rubbish, please?'

Reg Pengelly

Q: Why did the golfer wear an extra pair of trousers?

A: In case he got a hole in one.

Daphne Remington

Q: What do you call a cat who has eaten a duck?

A: A duck-filled fatty puss.

Liz Dixon

Q: Can a shoe box?

A: No, but a tin can.
Erich Wirtz

A sandwich walks into a bar. The barman says, 'Sorry, we don't serve food.'
Brian Palmer

Teacher: Simon, can you spell your name backwards
Simon: No mis

Simon

by Kirsten Nicolla Hill

Q: What did the earwig say as it fell down the stairs?

A: Ear we go, ear we go, ear we go . . .
Bernard Tate

A few months ago we were having a celebratory dinner at my father-in-law's. His wife is the most spectacular cook and we always looked forward to a visit. Our four-year-old son Thomas also joined us at the regal dining-room table with cut glasses, napkins and silver service. When the starter was served – prawn cocktail with crisp salad, drizzled with Thousand Island dressing – Nanna knew that Thomas would not enjoy it, so instead she had provided him with a warm crusty cob and best butter. Thomas took one look at his plate and then at ours, and said, 'Where's my plate of sick then?' There was a stunned silence, followed by much laughter. The story has already been repeated many times, and I'm sure Thomas will be reminded of it until he's at least twenty-one.

Rachel Hankinson

Our ice-cream man was found lying dead on the floor of his van, covered in nuts and hundreds-and-thousands. Police say he topped himself.

Brian Palmer

A man walked into a bar, sat down, and ordered a beer. As he sipped the beer, he heard a soothing voice say, 'Nice tie!' Looking around the bar he noticed that the place was empty except for himself and the barman. A few sips later the voice said, 'Beautiful shirt!' At this, the man called the barman over and said, 'I think I must be losing my mind – I keep hearing voices saying nice things, but there's nobody else here.'

'It's the peanuts,' answered the barman. 'They're complimentary!'

Peter Sugre

My three-year-old son was re-enacting the scene from *The Wind in the Willows* where Rat takes Mole boating for the first time. He pronounced that he was Ratty, and my wife was to be Mole. I enquired as to what my role would be. The reply, after much thought and a studied look, came thus: 'You can be the picnic basket.'

Philip Jobling

Q: Where does a sheep get its hair cut?

A: At the baabaa's.

Charlie Skidmore (age five)

A mummy snake and a baby snake were going through the jungle. The baby snake said, 'Mummy, am I one of those snakes that crush people or one that bites people and poisons them?'

'Why?' asked his mum.

The baby snake gave her a worried look and said,

'Because I've just bitten my tongue.'

Helen Hepworth

Q: How do crazy people go through the forest?

A: They take the psycho path.

Frank Everett

A tortoise was walking across the garden when two snails jumped out from the cabbage patch in front of him. They slid up his shell, over on to his head, then pinched the lettuce leaf out of his mouth, before going back into the bushes. When the garden police arrived, they asked the upset tortoise, 'Could you give us a description of your attackers, sir?' The tortoise replied, 'No, I'm sorry but it all happened so fast.'

Clive Gilson

Q: Where do you take a sick horse?

A: The horsepital.

Sue Edwards

My three-year-old daughter Shauna asked if she could go out to play one day. When I said, 'No, because the boys are too rough,' her instant reply was, 'If I can find a smooth one, then can I play?'

David Davies

One afternoon, to the amazement of the
librarian, a chicken walked into the library,
chose and checked out two books, then left
with one under each wing. An hour later,
the chicken returned the books, picked up
two more books, checked them out and left.
After another hour had passed, the same
thing happened, and this time the mystified
librarian decided to follow the bird after it
had left the library.

The chicken went to the local park and stopped at the duck pond, where there was a frog sitting on a lily pad.
The librarian watched as the chicken went over to the frog.
'Buk?' said the chicken.
'Reddit,' replied the frog.

Tracy Truelove

Q: What do you get if you cross an orchestra with a tyre factory?

A: Rubber bands.

Robin Vanags

Q: Which city is a very dangerous city?

A: Electricity.

Paul Jackson

In the early 1950s a friend of mine went back to work in what was then a rare factory that had a nursery. Her son was a 'tweeny' up to his fourth birthday, after which he became a 'toddler'. Following his birthday-party weekend, he came home on the Monday evening absolutely exhausted. When he collapsed into a chair and his mummy asked him why he was so tired, back came the reply: 'Mummy, you don't know the sponsorlolities we toddlers have looking after those tiresome tweenies!'

I am now seventy-five years old and I still have problems saying 'responsibilities'.

Marjorie Gorton

Q: Why did the orange stop in the middle of the road?

A: Because it ran out of juice.

Becky L. Morgan (age ten) and Sheila in Somerset

Q: How does an eskimo build his house?

A: Igloos it together.

Alan Aldridge

One day, Kevin's father was called in to
school to see the Headmaster.
'What's the problem?' he asked.
'Has Kevin done something wrong?'
'He certainly has,' said the Headmaster.
'He peed in the swimming pool.'
'Oh, come on,' said Kevin's dad. 'That's not
so bad. Lots of kids pee in swimming pools.'
The Headmaster sighed, and replied, 'Not
from the top diving board, they don't.'

Thomas Parrish (age eight)

Q: Why did the boy study in
the aeroplane?

A: He wanted a higher education.

Bernard Tate

When my youngest daughter Georgina, now aged nine, was much younger, we had to admit my husband to hospital. She sat on my lap as the nurse was going through the usual questions regarding age and so forth. 'Any caps or crowns?' she asked.

'No,' replied my husband.

Georgie whispered in my ear, 'Silly lady! Doesn't she know he's not a real king?'

Becky Jeffrey

Q: What do you call a skeleton when it doesn't get up in the morning?

A: Lazy bones.

Jay Todd

Q: What do you get if you lock a rabbit in a sauna?

A: A hot cross bunny.

Maggie Wells

When I was visiting my grandson Louis the other evening, he was busy colouring in and humming a little tune as he worked. 'I'm hummeling,' he explained. This instantly became a family word for humming. It obviously runs in the family, as his mother Eleisha joined us for Sunday lunch and the discussion turned to getting rid of bits and pieces at a car-boot sale. Eleisha stated that she couldn't do that. 'The trouble with me,' she said, 'is that I'm just too sementimental.' Enough said!

Beverley Hughes

Q: What do you call something purple that swings through vineyards?

A: Tarzan the Grapeman.

Helen Green

An inflatable boy went to an inflatable school where there were inflatable teachers and inflatable children. One day he got really fed up and decided to take a pin to school. He ended up bursting the school, the teachers, the children, the Headmaster and then himself. The Headmaster called him in to his office and said to the naughty schoolboy, 'I'm really annoyed with you. You've let the school down, you've let your friends down, you've let me down and, worst of all, you've let yourself down.'

Ken, Ali, Zoe and Holly

My granddaughter Sarah, aged three, was having her tea one day, which consisted of a sandwich and a bag of crisps. She picked the crisps from a big box of assorted snacks that we keep in the kitchen and, after a minute or two, I noticed that although the bag was open she wasn't actually eating the crisps. I also noticed that they were the super-hot chilli-flavour variety that I kept aside for her dad. 'What's wrong with your crisps, Sarah?' I asked.

'They're too hot, Granddad,' she replied.

'Why don't you get another packet then?' I suggested.

'It's all right,' she said. 'I'll wait for these to cool down.'

Chris Pocock

Q: Why do bagpipers walk when they play?

A: To get away from the noise.

Fred Clevett

Q: What goes 'zub zub'?

A: A bee flying backwards.

Joseph Mallows

Q: What do you call a man with jelly, fruit and custard in his ears?

A: Anything you like, he's a trifle deaf.

Chris Bryant

A penguin went into a bar and ordered a drink. The barman served him. After some time, the penguin called the barman over and asked, 'Have you seen my brother?' The barman thought for a moment and replied, 'I don't think so, what does he look like?'

Stephen Edwards

Q: What do you get when you cross a snowman with a vampire?

A: Frostbite.

Carol James

My daughter Topaz, aged four, spent New Year's Eve with her nanna, and they were discussing her great-nanna. 'Nanna, is Great-Nanna Yvonne dead?' she asked.

'Yes,' replied my mother-in-law.

'Is she in Heaven?' Topaz enquired. Again the affirmative followed from my mother-in-law. 'How did she get there?' was my daughter's reply.

My mother-in-law had to pause for a moment – 'Jesus took her,' she replied.

'How did he take her when he can't even drive?' Topaz asked. Later in the day, Topaz was asked by her uncle how she knew that Jesus couldn't drive. 'Don't be silly,' she replied. 'Of course he can't – he's only a baby. He was born last week!'

Sarah Ladbrook

Q: What happened to the frog that broke down?

A: It got toad away.

Chris Chapman

39

why does a giraffe have a long neck?

Anwser: so he can't smell his smelly feet.

By Geoffrey cheah

I'm 9 years old

Q: What did one strawberry say to the other strawberry?

A: If we hadn't been in the same bed we wouldn't be in this jam.

Chris Hinds

Q: What did the snake say to his girlfriend after an argument?

A: C'mon, let's hiss and make up.

Bernard Tate

Our four-year-old grandson George has an imaginary friend called Marcus, whom he calls his ghost friend. We were talking to George about Marcus, and asked him if he was a good ghost friend or a naughty one. He replied, 'Oh, he's very naughty.'

A couple of weeks later we took George out for the day. On the way home I could hear George chattering in the back seat of the car. 'What did you say, George?' I asked him.

He replied, 'I'm talking to Marcus, he's sitting beside me.'

My wife looked round and said, 'Marcus isn't wearing his seatbelt.'

George promptly responded, 'I told you he was naughty!'

Bill and Barbara Bell

Q: What's round and very bad-tempered?

A: A vicious circle.

Hilary Deadman

One morning a teacher told his class to take a pencil and paper, and write an essay with the title 'If I Were A Millionaire'. Everyone began to write furiously, apart from Philip, who leaned back with his arms folded. 'What's the matter, why don't you begin writing?' asked the teacher.

'I'm waiting for my secretary,' replied Philip.

Mr and Mrs L. Rowe

Q: Why did the farmer win the Nobel Prize?

A: Because he was out standing in his field.

Vicky Davies

Q: Why can't a steam engine sit down?

A: Because it has a tender behind.

Kirstine Drysdale

Did you hear about the fight in a biscuit tin? The Bandit hit the Yo~Yo with a Club, tied it up in a Blue Riband and got away in a Taxi.

Chris and Malcolm Dipple

I used to help run a youth group for eight- to eleven-year-olds. At a family service in the local church, a couple were having their little girl christened. I told the ten-year-old sitting beside me to listen carefully to the baby's name, as they were calling it after a gate that used to be part of the newly demolished Berlin Wall. He replied incredulously in a loud voice, 'What – Checkpoint Charlie?'

Rod Sutton

Q: Where do baby monkeys sleep in the jungle?

A: In ape~ri~cots.

Diz Dexter

Q: What's round and green,
and goes camping?

A: A boy sprout.

Di Kettle

Q: What do you call André Previn
vacuuming at midnight?

A: Orchestral man hoovers in the dark.

Michaela Halse

A few weeks ago our granddaughter Celine, aged seven, was taken to visit her other grandmother's grave in the local cemetery. The gravestone was very simple, with just the name and dates of her gran's birth and death. Celine looked at it and asked her mum, 'Is that Granny's phone number? Can I ring her when we get home?'

Ann and Colin Gage

Q: What's the difference between roast
chicken and pea soup?

A: You can roast chicken, but you can't
pee soup.

Gareth Lord (age ten)

Q: Why do elephants use green umbrellas?

A: So they can hide on snooker tables.

Have you ever seen an elephant
on a snooker table?
Good camouflage, isn't it?

Derek French

Q: What do sea monsters eat?
A: Fish and ships.

Frank Everett and Evelyn Salmon

'Doctor, doctor, I can't stop singing "The Green, Green Grass of Home".'

'That sounds like Tom Jones Syndrome.'

'Is it common?'

'It's not unusual.'

Brian Palmer

My granddaughter Imogen, aged four, was ready to go to a fancy-dress party dressed as a fairy, complete with tiara and wand. I asked her whether she had tried out her wand to see if it worked. 'Grandpa,' she said, giving me a somewhat puzzled look, 'it's not a real one!'

Brian C. Edgill

Q: What do you call a man wearing paper underpants?

A: Russell.

Margaret Williams

When working as a nanny in the early 1980s, I collected one of my charges, Richard, from playgroup. I asked him what he'd been doing all day and, after the usual rundown of craft activities, playing and singing, we eventually came to the story. When I asked what the story was about, he said, 'Cheeses.'

I said, 'Cheeses?'

'Yes, cheeses,' he said.

'What about cheeses?' I asked.

The reply came, 'You know, baby cheeses in the Bible.'

Joy Savill

Two butterflies went to a dance, but they couldn't get in – it was a moth ball.

Richard Learman

A man who was going to a fancy-dress party put on a Somerset smock, a yokel hat and picked up a shepherd's crook. 'You going as a farmer, then?' asked his friend.
'No, I'm a spy,' replied the man.
'To be a spy you need a black pointed hat, a black cape and a round black bomb with a fuse stuck in it,' said his friend.
'No, not that sort of spy,' laughed the man, shaking his head. 'I'm a shepherd's pie.'

Paul Leavett

Q: What do you call a judge with no thumbs?

A: Justice Fingers.

Pip Standford

Q: What did the big chimney say to the little chimney?

A: You're too young to smoke.

Roger Giles

A few months ago I took my four-year-old son Miles to see our family doctor, as he had been suffering with a persistent cough. My other son Guy, who is five and a half, also came along. The doctor examined Miles thoroughly, and looked in his ears and down his throat while Guy stood watching with great interest. The doctor turned to me and asked, 'Does he wheeze?' and before I could answer Guy piped up: 'Oh, yes! He wees on the carpet, in the car, on the sofa, in his shorts . . .'

Caroline Fintan

Q: What do you do if you break your leg in two places?
A: Don't go back to those two places.

Dawn

Two monkeys were sitting in the bath. One said to the other, 'Ooh ooh ooh, ah ah ah!' The other one replied, 'All right then, I'll put some cold water in.'

Pete Donovan

Q: What do you do if you see a spaceman?

A: Park in it, man.

Alison Moore

Our grandson George, aged four, was staying with us one day and was picking at his dinner. My wife said to him, 'Come on, George, eat your dinner.'

He replied, 'I'm not hungry.'

'I bet you eat your dinner at nursery,' my wife continued, persistently.

'Oh yes,' he said, 'we get told off if we don't eat it.'

My wife replied, 'OK, George, I'll pretend to be your teacher and tell you to eat your dinner.'

'OK,' he said, 'and I'll pretend to eat it!'

Bill and Barbara Bell

Q: What do you call a chicken
in a shellsuit?

A: An egg.
Wendy Ashman and Wendy Turner

Two cannibals were having dinner. One said
to the other, 'I hate my mother-in-law.'
'Never mind,' said the other one,
'just eat your veg.'
Toby Langford

Q: What did the traffic light say
to the motor car?

A: Don't look while I change.
Bernard Tate

Q: What kind of shoes do teddies wear?

A: None, they've got bear feet.
Lindsay Dryburgh

When I was three years old I caught a bus on my own. It was going from Buxton to Tideswell in Derbyshire. Although I had managed to climb aboard the bus, my parents and my baby brother hadn't been able to get on as it was so full. After about a mile, the conductress realized I was all on my own and so the bus was stopped at a pub where I was collected by a policeman. When he asked me where I lived, I said, 'Next to Mabel,' which was true, but not very helpful. I am forty-seven now and can remember it all very vividly!

Karen Wolle

Q: Why do bumblebees always look so pretty?
A: Because they use honey-combs.

Diane

Q: What do dinosaurs put on their chips?

A: Tomatosaurus.

Ann Towriss

Two eskimos were sitting in their canoe feeling very cold, so they decided to light a fire to get warm. The fire burned a hole in the bottom of the canoe, and they all sank. Moral: You can't have your kayak and heat it.

Chris Ellis

by Rachel Huang
Age 10   65

Q: Who wrote the book entitled 'I Fell Off A Cliff?

A: Eileen Dover.

Pam Wornham

Many years ago when my daughter was only two, I was living in Cramlington. There was a small charity shop in the town that sold mainly children's clothes. At the time parka coats were very popular and I bought Ann one for only 20p! She was very proud of her parka and liked to wear it all the time. One day while we passed through the village on a crowded bus, she suddenly pointed to the shop and shouted, 'Mummy! There's the shop where we bought my coat.' I never dreamed that a two-year-old would be capable of embarrassing me so completely in front of a whole busful of people.

Janice Clough

Q: What do you get when you cross a parrot with a centipede?

A: A walkie-talkie.

John McMahon

Q: Why did the toilet paper go down the hill?

A: To get to the bottom.

Amyleigh Watts

Q: What do you call an eight-sided cat?

A: An octopus.

James Robinson

Q: How many elephants can you get
in a Mini?

A: Two in the front and two in the back.

Q: How many hippos can you get in a Mini?

A: You can't – there are already four
elephants in there.

Tom Jones

'Knock, knock.'
'Who's there?'
'Boo.'
'Boo who?'
'There's no need to cry.'

Ginny from Bristol

Two peanuts walk into a bar.
One was a salted.

Brian Palmer

One Saturday afternoon the six-year-old son of a friend of mine announced, 'I'm leaving!' Clutching a pillowcase filled with biscuits, some fruit and his favourite cuddly toy, he left. His mother remained calm and rang the neighbours to ask them to keep an eye on him, but not to interfere as he walked by, while her husband went quietly into nervous collapse. As the boy wandered slowly down the road, an hour passed, then two, at which point my friend received a phone call from a neighbour who said, 'He's coming back your way!' A little while later the door opened, and the youngster walked into the living room where his parents were sitting, trying to look calm. The boy put his hands on his hips and announced, 'All right – I'll give you one more chance!'

Blodget

Q: Why have elephants got big ears?

A: Because Noddy won't pay the ransom.

Kathy Prewings

Did you hear about the magic tractor?
It turned into a field.

Andy Bonney

When my son Tom was an infant, he was a very enthusiastic, confident and happy child. Life was always fun and challenging. He loved to go to school, and when I met him at the infant-school gates at three in the afternoon, he would usually tell me what a happy day he'd had. One day, he came out of school, excited as usual, and very pleased to tell me of his day's triumphs. 'Mummy,' he said, 'I've been playing tennis today. I'm very good at it too.'

'That's lovely,' I replied.

'Yes,' he said. 'I'm not very good at hitting the ball, but I'm very good at everything else.' What a blissful view of life at the tender age of five!

Jean Weeks

Q: What do you call a dinosaur with no eyes?

A: A Do~you~think~he~saurus.

Did you know it also had a dog?

It's called
Do~you~think~he~saurus~Rex.

Steve and Lorna Froggatt, and Jean Chetcuti

Q: Why is the sky so high?

A: So the birds don't bump their heads.

Oliver Sharpe (age twelve)

Q: What do you call a cow that cuts the grass?

A: A lawn moo~er.

James Husain (age fifteen)

After having just moved house, my wife had to make numerous trips into town, dragging our reluctant five-year-old with her. She had decided to buy herself a piano for our new home, and on the day that my wife intended to go and purchase the instrument, our daughter asked, 'Mummy, why are we going into town again?'

When my wife told her they were off to buy a piano, our daughter replied, 'Well, I hope you don't expect me to carry it!'

Nick Wyatt

Q: Why do witches ride broomsticks?

A: Because vacuum cleaners are too heavy.
Jen Lucas

Q: What do you get if you cross a hen
with a banjo?

A: A self-plucking chicken.
John Marsh

Q: What do you call a woman with a boat on her head?

A: Maude.

Helen Green

A man went to his doctor and said, 'On Monday I felt like Mickey Mouse, on Tuesday I felt like Donald Duck and on Wednesday I felt like Pluto.'
The doctor replied, 'Tell me, how long have you been having these Disney spells?'

Stinus Andersen

I was on holiday once with my daughter and granddaughter Polly, who was then aged four and a half. One afternoon, while Polly and her mum stayed by the pool, I went back to our room. I had left the door open deliberately, and when they returned Polly explained that it wasn't safe to leave doors open. I said, 'No one would want an old woman like me,' to which Polly replied, 'You don't know, Grandma. He could be blind or have lost his way!'

Dot Alexander

Q: What is stupid and yellow?

A: Thick custard.

Kate Harris

Q: Who designed Noah's Ark?

A: An ark~itect.

Bernard Tate

A schoolteacher in Newcastle asked her pupils to use the word 'fascinate' in a sentence. Molly said, 'My family went to granddad's farm and we saw all his pet sheep. It was fascinating.'

The teacher replied, 'That was good, but I wanted you to use the word "fascinate".'

Sally raised her hand and called out, 'My mum and dad took me to the Natural History Museum and I was fascinated.'

The teacher said, 'Well, that was good too, Sally, but I really want to hear

the word "fascinate" by itself.'
When Thomas raised his hand the teacher
hesitated, as the youngster was noted for
his bad language. However, she decided to
give him a chance, and listened in
frustration as Thomas said, 'My mum has a
sweater with ten buttons, but because
she's so fat, she can only fasten eight.'

Ian Edwards

Q: What do you get if you cross an
elephant with a goldfish?

A: Swimming trunks.

Anonymous

My wife usually cuts my hair (what's left of it),
and when the weather is nice she does it in the
garden. When our grandson George was two,
he was averse to having his hair cut, and on one
occasion he was kicking up such a fuss, so I
said to him, 'George, I had my hair cut this
morning. Guess where I had it done?'

He replied, 'Down the middle.'

Bill and Barbara Bell

Q: What do you get if you cross a pop star with a biscuit?

A: A Lionel Rich Tea.

Emma Love

A two-and-a-half-year-old girl walked into the bathroom while her mother was putting on make-up. 'I'm going to look just like you, Mummy,' she announced.

'Maybe, when you grow up,' said her mother.

'No, Mummy, by tomorrow,' replied her daughter. 'I just put on that Oil of Old Lady you always use.'

Michael Bentley

Q: Why do you have to tiptoe past the medicine cabinet?

A: So you don't wake the sleeping pills.

Karen Cocking

What did the big tomato say to the small tomato?
You run ahead and I'll Ketchup.

By Ruth Andrews

Q: What do you call two robbers?

A: A pair of knickers.

Liz Duncan

My granddaughter had been watching a pet-rescue programme on television, after which she had a conversation with her dad.

'Daddy, I don't want to be an animal doctor when I grow up,' she said.

'Why is that?' he enquired.

She replied, 'Because the animal doctor's got a beard, and I'm a girl!'

Wendy Somers

Q: What do you get if you cross a skunk with an owl?

A: An animal that smells terrible, but doesn't give a hoot.

Jack Eadie

Teacher: Thomas, do you know the difference between a buffalo and a bison?

Thomas: Yes miss, you can't wash your hands in a buffalo.

Steve Bowen

Our five-year-old, Zoë, commented the other day that she liked the TV weather forecast because it showed where the toilets were. Her mum, Marion, was intrigued by this remark, and watched avidly to see what her daughter could mean. When it was over, Zoë said, 'There weren't any toilets today, Mum.' Then, after a thoughtful pause, she asked, 'You do spell loo L-O-W, don't you?'

Chris Benton

A jump-lead walks into a bar.
The barman says, 'I'll serve you,
but don't start anything.'

Brian Palmer

Q: What do you call a zombie in a belfry?

A: A dead ringer.

Matt Hill

Our grandson George, aged four, who has an imaginary friend called Marcus, has been going through a phase of biting his nails, which I have had to chastise him about. A few days ago he came up to me and said, 'Look Granddad, I've stopped biting my nails.'

I looked at them, couldn't see much of an improvement, and so I said, 'No, you haven't.'

He replied, 'Yes I have, it's Marcus that's biting them, 'cos he's four now.'

I asked where Marcus was, and George informed me, 'He's under the settee.'

'I'll have a word with him and tell him to stop biting your nails,' I said, to which George replied, 'You can't do that because he's had his ears chopped off.'

Bill and Barbara Bell

Q: Which knight invented the Round Table?

A: Sir Cumference.

Stephen Twiss

Q: How do you know if there's an elephant in bed with you?

A: By the 'E' on his pyjamas.

Ann Towriss

A small girl went in to a clock shop and told the shopkeeper that she had just started school and needed a 'potato clock'. The shopkeeper replied that he had never heard of such a thing, and asked her how she knew that she needed a potato clock. 'Well,' said the girl, 'my teacher says I have to be at school every day at nine, so I have to get up~at~eight~o'clock.'

Stephen Oswald

One day, when my mother-in-law was trying to teach her second daughter, Jane, to count, she picked out four Smarties and placed them in Jane's open hand one by one. 'One, two, three and one more makes four Smarties,' she said. 'Now Jane, if I give you another Smartie, what will that make?'

Jane replied honestly, 'It'll make me very happy, Mummy.'

Andrew Fish

A man went to the doctor and said, 'Doctor, doctor, I feel like a pig.'
'And how long have you been feeling like this?' the doctor asked.
The man replied, 'About a weeeeeeeeek.'

Sandra Cosgrove

Q: What do you call a fly with no wings?

A: A walk.

Linda Wright

Q: What is red and sits in the corner?

A: A naughty bus.

Penny Aylwin

Q: What do you call a woman with a beer glass on her head?

A: Beatrix.

Zoë Fitzgerald-Pool

Q: What's the fastest fish in the river?

A: A motorpike.

Q: What's the second fastest fish
in the river?

A: A sidecarp.

The lads at SMS Earl's Court

One day my daughter Rosanna (now eleven) was at playschool learning about animals. The playschool leader held up a picture of a koala bear and asked the audience of four-year-olds what the animal was called. Rosanna, always keen, put up her hand and said, 'It's a koala bear, Miss.'

The lady replied, 'Well done, Rosanna – and do you know where it lives?'

'In Bristol Zoo, Miss,' said Rosanna.

The playschool leader held back a smirk, and said, 'Yes, you do get koala bears in zoos, but they also live in a place a long, long way away.'

Rosanna thought for a while and replied, 'Manchester, Miss.'

Andrew Fish

Q: Why did the parrot wear a raincoat?

A: Because he wanted to be polyunsaturated.

Stella Crowther

Q: What do you get when you cross a stereo with a fridge?

A: The coolest music in town.

Mike Hesp

Considering that I'm seventy-three, I thought the veins on the backs of my hands were not too bad, until my great-grandson Jak, aged six, asked me, 'What are those roots growing out of your hands for, Nan?'

Margaret from Warrington

Q: What do cows eat for breakfast?

A: Moo~sli.

Jack McNicoll

Q: What do you do if the M6 motorway is closed?

A: Go down the M3 twice.

Gareth Lord (age ten)

Q: Why didn't the bogey play football?

A: Because he wasn't picked.

Annie Eaton

How do fleas get from place to place?
By itch-hiking

Hee Joo 8 years

A man took his Rottweiler to the vet and said, 'My dog's cross-eyed. Is there anything you can do for him?'

'Well,' said the vet, 'let's take a look at him.' So the vet picked up the dog and examined his eyes, then checked his teeth. Finally, he concluded, 'I'm going to have to put him down.'

'What, because he's cross-eyed?' asked the man.

'No,' replied the vet. 'Because he's really heavy.'

Brian Palmer

I am a chemotherapy nurse at Addenbrooke's Hospital in Cambridge. One day, while watching the medical soap *Holby City* on TV, my five-year-old daughter Alice asked, 'Mummy, do you watch this so you know what to do when you're at work?'

Joanne Crofts

Q: What did the fish say when it swam into the wall?

A: Dam.

Adele Swift (age seven) and Brian Palmer (Fiona's dad)

Q: How do you get milk from a cat?

A: Take away its saucer.

Jane Andrews

My son Andrew went walkabout when he was three years old. A determined little boy, he climbed a six-foot fence, walked along a main road, crossed another main road and went to his five-year-old sister's school. He must have journeyed there at the speed of an Olympian, as it was only a matter of minutes before I noticed he wasn't in the enclosed garden. The police were called and we were all on red alert, and I was a total wreck when the school rang. Andrew had gone straight to his sister's classroom and sat down to join the lesson. He must be one of the few children who have run away to school instead of from it.

Paula Finney

Q: What do you call a rabbit that does a lot of exercise, and a rabbit with a flower in its mouth?

A: One is a fit bunny and the other is a bit funny.

Elaine Gunns

Q: What's big, red and eats rocks?

A: A big, red rock~eater.

Nicholas Ducker

'Doctor, doctor, every time I drink my tea I get a pain in my right eye.'
'Have you tried taking the spoon out of the cup first?'

Janie Drury

Q: What do frogs drink?

A: Croak-a-Cola.

Di Kettle

Q: Why did the gardener plant bulbs?

A: So that worms could see in the dark.

Katherine Haxton

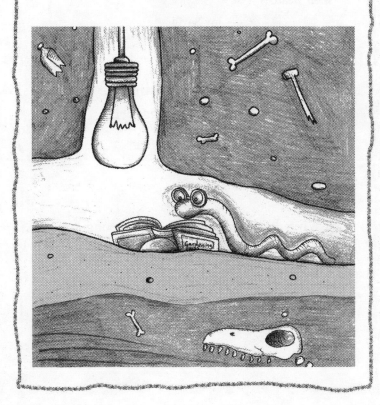

When my son Alexander was about three, he asked me when we were going to see Granddad Hair. I had an idea he meant my father, as he was the only one of Alexander's granddads who was not bald and, after checking, I was proved right. I asked him why he called his granddad by that name, and he replied, 'All my other granddads have body growing through their heads!'

Joy Savill

Q: What do Scottish people have for dessert?

A: Tartan custard.

Steve Gibbons

Q: Why does a flamingo lift up one leg?

A: Because if he lifted up both legs he would fall over.

Hannah Dunton (age six)

Q: What do you do if you get a peanut stuck in your ear?

A: Pour in some melted chocolate and it will come out a Treat.

Wendy Turner

Q: What did one fish say to his friend in the tank?

A: How do you drive this thing then?

Michelle Huntley

Our grandson George, aged three, was scribbling on a piece of paper on a card table at his great-grandma's house. To protect the baize cloth she passed him a magazine and said, 'George, rest on that.' He promptly put his left elbow on it, rested his head in his hand and carried on writing.

Bill and Barbara Bell

When my son Peter was two and a half years old, I used to work on the buses in Plymouth with my cousin, Derek, who was living with us at the time. One day we were both on the two-to-ten shift, and dinner was at lunchtime and had to be on the table promptly so that we could both get to work on time. My wife Maureen had cooked a wonderful roast beef meal with all the trimmings, including Yorkshire puds as tall as skyscrapers. Pete was out playing, so she dished up our food and told us to carry on while she went out to get him.

Derek and I tucked in, both attacking our huge, crispy Yorkshire puddings simultaneously, but a second later, still in unison, we were both compelled to spit out the vilest-tasting thing we had ever eaten. When Maureen returned with Peter and saw the pile of half-chewed Yorkshire pudding on the table, she was understandably annoyed. However, we persuaded her to try a mouthful as well, which quickly ended up with the other two rejected morsels of inedible food. She started to investigate the cause of the terrible taste and noticed that the soapdish on the kitchen draining board was empty. What we soon realized was that our sweet little Pete had climbed up to the worktop, where the mixture was standing in a bowl, and he had simply dropped in the soap. A final whisk prior to baking had ensured the soapy taste had spread throughout the mixture!

Mick Jeffs

Q: What do you call a man
hanging on a wall?

A: Art.

Zoe Fitzgerald-Pool

Q: Why do cows have bells?

A: Because their horns don't work.

Haig Parry, and Norman of Pyrford

Q: Why did the strawberry cry?

A: Because his parents were in a jam.

Peter Whitesmith

Q: What's green and has wheels?

A: Grass. I lied about the wheels.

Diane Weber

Q: What do jelly babies wear in the rain?

A: Gum boots.

Kirsty

Q: What is the connection between Henry the Eighth and Kermit the Frog?

A: They both have the same middle name.

Ann Mason

Q: Why didn't the skeleton cross the road?

A: Because he didn't have the guts.

Danny Walker (age ten)

Q: What do you call a woodpecker without a beak?

A: A headbanger.

Bob Clarke

My two-and-a-half-year-old daughter was recently looking at a photograph of my dear departed mother. 'Who's that?' she asked.

'It's Mummy's mummy, your grandma,' I replied.

'Where is she?' asked my daughter.

'Grandma is with the angels in the sky,' I said.

My daughter thought for a moment and then asked, 'Is she an astronaut, Mummy?'

Ali McArthur

Q: What do you call a teacher with no arms, no legs and no body?

A: The Head.

Murray Robinson (age seven)

Q: How do you tell the difference between a weasel and a stoat?

A: Well, it's weasily done because they're stoatily different.

John Merritt

Q: What do you call a Roman emperor with flu?

A: Julius Sneezer.

Helen Green

Q: What is a witch's favourite subject at school?

A: Spelling.

Sue Weaver

My granddaughter Polly, aged four, was returning home one dark evening with her mother, who used to work as an air stewardess. Polly looked at the sky, saw an aircraft and said, 'I wish I could go in a plane every day.'

Her mother answered, 'That's strange, Polly, I used to fly every day.'

'Were you with the man in the front?' Polly asked.

My daughter said 'no' and before she could continue Polly replied, 'Oh, you were the dinner lady!'

Dot Alexander

Q: What is gram scared of?

A: A killer gram.

Don Payne

Q: What do you call a sheep with no legs?

A: A cloud.

Duncan Borland

Q: Why don't oysters give to charity?

A: Because they are shellfish.

Chris Lewis

Q: Where do all the policemen live?

A: Letsby Avenue.

Chris McAllister

Q: What's yellow and dangerous?

A: Shark~infested custard.

Belinda

'Knock, knock.'

'Who's there?'

'A little boy.'

'A little boy who?'

'A little boy who can't reach the doorbell.'

Mick Stoner

When my late husband was small, he fell out with his parents and packed his small brown suitcase, just like the one belonging to Paddington Bear, before setting off . . . to sit in the cupboard under the stairs. Lunchtime came and went – no talk of a lost child – teatime came and went. Then his father opened the cupboard door and said, 'Time for bed, son.' When my husband grew up he became a police officer, and whenever he had to look for lost children, the first place he looked was the cupboard under the stairs – he found many that way.

Jemma Jenks

Q: Why aren't there any aspirin in the jungle?

A: Because the parrots~eat~'em~all.

Morwenna

Q: Where do you weigh a whale?

A: At a whale weigh station.

Lynn M.

Q: What do you call a bear with no ears?

A: B.

Jessica Hall

Q: What do snowmen have for breakfast?

A: Snowflakes.

Mark Drury (age four)

When my granddaughter Sian was two, she was having a race with her mum in the garden. They stood at the top of the garden, and I called out, 'Ready . . . Steady . . .' and before I could say 'Go,' Sian shouted out, 'Cook!' She obviously watches too much daytime television.

Wendy Somers

Q: What says 'tick, tick, woof?

A: Not a watchdog, but a dog
marking homework.

Wombat in Sweden

Q: What do you get if you cross two
elephants with a fish?

A: A pair of swimming trunks.

Rebecca May Taphouse (age three)

When my daughter Rebecca was three, I was
sitting in the car with her, waiting for my mum
who had popped to the shops. As usual Rebecca
climbed into the front, and we began playing 'I
Spy' to pass the time. After I'd had my go,
Rebecca thought of something beginning with
'P' and she said it was inside the car. I struggled
for a bit and then asked her for a clue. She
leaned across and ran her chubby fingers
around the steering wheel. 'It's inside there,' she
said. I looked at her blankly, gave up and asked
her for the answer, which was, 'Peep, peep!'

Chris Burrows

Q: There are two mice in the airing cupboard; which one is in the army?

A: The one sat on the tank.

Mark Powell

Q: Why couldn't the sailors play cards?

A: Because the captain was standing on the deck.

Suyin Powell

Q: Where do you find giant snails?

A: At the end of giants' fingers.

William Boyce

'Knock, knock.'
'Who's there?'
'Canoe.'
'Canoe who?'
'Canoe help me with my homework?'

Akihiko Tse (age eight)

Many years ago I lived in Malawi, and one day I went to a friend's house for coffee. I was eight months' pregnant at the time, and brought out the baby jacket I was knitting. My friend told her four-year-old son that I had a baby in my tummy, and that I was knitting the jacket for the baby. He looked very puzzled, and asked me, 'Are you going to eat the jacket so that the baby can put it on?'

Moira Harris

'Knock, knock.'

'Who's there?'

'Lettuce.'

'Lettuce who?'

'Lettuce in, it's raining.'

Sally Yuen Wing (age nine)

Q: What do you get if you cross a cow with a camel?

A: Lumpy milkshakes.

Jenny Morris

Q: What do you get if you cross a mouse with an elephant?

A: Great big holes in the skirting board.

Mike Bedrock

A number of years ago my sister and her husband were living in Bath, and my sister had just produced son number four, Oliver. Being the only aunt, I had gone to inspect the new arrival. My sister was sitting in the lounge, breastfeeding young Oliver, and being closely watched by son number three, Nick, who was about four at the time. After much thought, Nick suddenly came out with, 'Is Oliver going to eat Aunty Jane next?' Poor Nick couldn't understand what we found so funny.

Jane Skentelbery

Q: Who earns a living driving their customers away?

A: A taxi driver.

Molly Barnes

Q: What is a physicist's favourite meal?

A: Fission chips.

Eric Martin

Q: Which town ties up its meat in strong twine?

A: Nottingham.

Thomas Knowles (age three)

'Doctor, doctor, I feel like an apple.'
'Well, come in – I won't bite you.'

Beatrice Malupa

Q: Why are goldfish orange?

A: The water makes them rusty.

Alison Flowers

When my grandson Jackson was two, his mum took him to visit an aunt. While he was playing he made a rude noise, whereupon his mum said, 'Well, what do you say?'

Jackson looked at his aunty and said, 'Thank you for having me!'

Judy Linnell

Q: What is an ig?

A: An eskimo's house with no loo.

Alison Wright

Q: Who held the baby octopus to ransom?

A: Squidnappers.

Chloë Farmer

Q: Why are fish so clever?

A: Because they live in schools.

Tony Parker

Two boiled eggs were bobbing about alongside each other in a pan of boiling water. One egg said to the other, 'Gosh, it's jolly hot in here.' The second egg replied, 'Wait until you get out – you get your head smashed in!'

Kay and Sid Holden, and Rob Urquhart

Two children went into a pet shop and said
to the man behind the counter, 'We'd like
to buy a wasp, please.'
'I'm sorry, we don't sell wasps,'
replied the man.
The children piped up, 'But you've got
one in the window.'

Abigail and Joseph Hitchins (age six and four)

Several years ago we went to stay with my mother for a few days. One morning my mother asked my daughter, who was then about four years old, if she was going to have a wash. My daughter replied in a puzzled tone, 'What for? You don't get dirty in bed!'

Mike Pyman

Q: Why didn't the skeleton go to the party?

A: He had no body to go with.

Emma Hazelgrove and Natalie Cotts

Q: How did your mum know that you hadn't washed your face?

A: I forgot to wet the soap.

Henry Baker

Q: What's a cat's favourite cereal?

A: Mice crispies.

Oliver (age nine)

Several four-year-olds in my school were talking about baby animals. 'What is a baby pig called?' asked their teacher.

'A piglet,' they replied confidently.

'Well, what do we call a baby cow?' she continued.

'A calf,' they said happily.

'And what is a baby deer called?'

After a short pause, a little voice piped up, 'Darling?'

Katie Lane

Q: Why did the cat cross the road?

A: Because he lived in the meows.

Cara Hodgson-Reed

Q: What kind of dog has a fever?

A: A hot dog.

Adele Quinton-Page (age nine)

Why was Cinderella thrown out of the netball team?
Because she kept running away from the ball.

 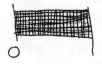

By Kathryn Clayton

When my daughter Emma was five she decided to run away from home, never to return. She packed a bag, took some tins of food so that she wouldn't be hungry and said goodbye. As we lived at the bottom of a hill in the middle of fields, I watched her climb up the hill. When she got about halfway up she stopped, opened the bag and took out a tin of something. Then she started back down the hill. I thought she had simply calmed down, but when she got to the front door she knocked and very politely asked if she could borrow a tin opener!

Diana Owen

Doctor: What do you do for a living?

Patient: I'm a magician.

Doctor: That's unusual.
What's your best trick?

Patient: I saw a woman in half.

Doctor: And is that very difficult?

Patient: No, it's child's play. I learned to
do it when I was a boy.

Doctor: Have you any brothers or sisters?

Patient: I have two half-sisters.

Sue Newman and James Hinchliffe

Q: What do you get when you cross a dog
with an elephant?

A: A very nervous postman.

James Elliott (age six) and John Farmer

On a visit to our home in Reading, my mother agreed to look after her grandchildren, aged five and three, while we enjoyed an evening out. Her granddaughter, a rather touchy child, decided that Granny was not going to do as requested and told her to go back home. When Granny explained to her that it was rather a long way to go back home to Inverness, the retort was, 'Well, you can go to the bottom of the garden instead!'

Alastair Smith

Q: What do you call a gorilla with bananas in its ears?

A: Anything you like – it can't hear you.

David Frame

Q: What sound do porcupines make when they kiss?

A: Ouch.

Penny Johnson

Q: What has six legs and flies?

A: A witch giving her cat a ride.

Rupert Osbourne

Q: Which award could be given to the inventor of the door knocker?

A: The 'no-bell' prize.

Peggy Kieser

One day, when my daughter Laura was a toddler, she had been running round the house so much that her socks had fallen down. She came up to me and said, 'Daddy, pull my socks up.'

I was slightly disappointed not to get a 'please', so I said, 'Daddy, pull my socks up what?' To which she replied, in a tone that suggested I was completely stupid, 'Up my leg.'

John Fedorowycz

Q: How can you tell if a corpse is angry?

A: It flips its lid.

Simon Thompson

Q: Why should you always take a mushroom to a party?

A: Because he's a fun~gi to be with.

Charlotte Ilett

'Knock, knock.'

'Who's there?'

'Mayonnaise.'

'Mayonnaise who?'

'Mayonnaise have seen the glory of the coming of the Lord.'

Chris Smith

Q: Why was the ghost of Anne Boleyn always running after the ghost of Henry the Eighth?

A: She was trying to get ahead.

Jane France

My nephew Matt showed real signs of being unable to take responsibility for his actions at the age of three. One afternoon he was playing with my son Jack under the coffee table in our lounge when Jack, aged seven, let out the most enormous wail. He came out holding his arm, saying that Matt had bitten him while playing. My sister Julie grabbed Matt from under the table, obviously extremely cross with him, apologized and took Matt home early to punish him. Most of the way home Matt was shouting and protesting that it really wasn't him who had bitten Jack. Being unable to take any more, Julie shouted, 'Well, if it wasn't you, who was it?' He shouted back, totally exasperated, 'It wasn't me, it was my naughty teeth!'

Karen Shields

Q: What do you call a werewolf that drinks too much?

A: A whino.

Fred Martin

Q: What were the gangster's last words?

A: Who put that violin in my violin case?

Benjamin Taylor

Q: What happened when someone kicked the blacksmith's dog?

A: It made a bolt for the door.

Eric Martin

Q: What do you call a boomerang that doesn't come back?

A: A stick.

Peter Cork

Q: What do elves do after school?

A: Gnomework.

Terry Porter

One of my favourite moments in teaching happened when I was with a class of six-year-olds who were supposed to be sitting quietly on the carpet, listening to me sharing words of wisdom with them. One little lad was clearly not impressed, and kept wriggling about, poking other children and generally being a distraction. After addressing many calm remarks at him – 'Sit down, Harry,' 'Hands in lap, Harry,' 'Try not to wriggle, Harry' – I was beginning to get a little exasperated. Finally, I turned round to look at him and said quite sharply, 'Harry, what can I say to make you listen to me?' and back came the muffled reply, 'Something interesting!'

Hazel Channon

While on holiday in Blackpool, my mother and father took my brother to visit the aquarium. After gazing at the monsters of the deep for a while, he skipped into the section that contained the rays, soles and other flatfish, where, much to the amusement of the other visitors, he called out excitedly, 'Look Daddy, these fish have been stepped on!'

Derrick Entwistle

Q: What is a baby's motto?
A: If at first you don't succeed, cry, cry again.

Linda Smith

Mother: Why did you just swallow the money I gave you?
Son: Well, you did say it was my lunch money.

John Jenkins

Q: Why did the mouse sit on the chair?
A: Because there was a cat sat
on the mat.

Cara Hodgson-Reed

My niece Jessica went to stay with my sister-in-law for the day. After Jessica had been there an hour she kept saying her feet were tired, so my sister-in-law asked Jessica what the reason was. Jessica replied, 'Because they woke up before me.'

Mary Richards

One day a boy with an ear infection is taken by his mum to see the doctor. The mother was very impressed with the way the doctor directed his questions at the lad. When he asked the boy, 'Is there anything you're allergic to?' the youngster turned to the doctor and whispered in his ear. Smiling, the doctor wrote out a prescription and handed it to the boy's mother. Without looking at it, she tucked it into her handbag.

Later, the pharmacist made up the pills and remarked on the unusual allergy her son must have. When he saw the mother's puzzled expression, he showed her the label on the bottle. As per the doctor's instructions, it said,

'Do not take with broccoli.'

Michael Bentley

Following the death of a dear friend many years ago, my husband and I were preparing to go to the funeral. Our daughter Sarah, then aged six, was intrigued and asked what a funeral was. I tried to tell her in very simple terms that Aunty was going to be buried, and that it meant that Aunty would go into the ground. Sarah replied quite innocently, 'Does that mean that Aunty will grow into a new Aunty, like a plant?'

Joan Bedo

Q: - Where do wasps live?

A: - Stingapore!!!

By Bonnie Lau, 9.

Q: Where do knights learn to kill dragons?

A: At knight school.

Lesley Kirby

When my son Nicholas was attending a Church of England infant school a few years ago, he ran outside one day in a very excited state because he had got a part in the Easter play. 'Mummy, Mummy, I'm half a tree!'

I felt quite despondent at the lack of a more sizeable role and asked him, 'Why couldn't you be a whole tree?'

Nicholas looked up at me and said, 'No, Mummy, I'm the offertory!'

Jacqui Gardener

A pretty girl walked up to the fabric counter in a department store and chose some cloth. 'I want to buy this material for a new dress,' she said.

'How much does it cost?'

'Only one kiss per yard,' replied the smirking male assistant.

'That's fine,' said the girl.

'I'll take ten yards.'

With expectation and anticipation written all over his face, the assistant quickly measured out and wrapped the material, then teasingly held it out to the girl. She snapped up the package and pointed to a little old man standing beside her.

'Grandpa will pay the bill,' she responded, smiling sweetly.

Rob Mellowship

On the beach one day, a little boy asked
his grandfather to kick his bucket.
Granddad asked, 'Why do you want me to
kick your bucket?'
'Because Mum said that when Granddad
kicks the bucket, I can have a new bike,'
the little boy replied.

Teresa Murchhill

My husband David, son of the local Welsh
Baptist minister, attended the birthday party of
one of the church member's children when he
was about five. The child's mother had
prepared a lovely tea for the children, who were
all tucking in to the goodies. Noticing that
David wasn't helping himself to any of the food,
the mother asked him if she could get him
anything. He replied, 'Yes, my coat – I want
to go home!' Needless to say, he was not
invited again.

Ann Tudno Williams

Q: What has forty feet and sings?

A: The school choir.

Nicola Carter

Mother: What did you learn
at school today?
Son: How to write.
Mother: What did you write?
Son: I don't know, they haven't taught us
how to read yet.

Imogen Sanders (age seven)

Q: Why is the fish shop always crowded?

A: Because the fish fillet.

Ian Rodger

Q: If Ireland sank into the sea, which
county wouldn't sink?

A: Cork.

Mark Hart

An elephant and a giraffe were at a waterhole having a drink. By their noses a turtle popped up out of the water, and the elephant's instant reaction was to stamp on it – splat! 'Why did you do that?' asked the giraffe, shocked.

'Twenty~five years ago, that same turtle came up out of the water at this very waterhole and bit my trunk – it began to bleed and was very painful.'

'My goodness,' said the giraffe. 'How did you remember it was the same one?'

'I have turtle recall,' said the elephant.

Keith

Two snowmen were talking. One said to the other, 'Can you smell carrots?'
Susan Clarkson

My partner Yvonne was once walking our daughter Sadie (who was two years old at the time) through the beautiful Victorian Leys Park in Matlock, Derbyshire. 'Do you know what these flowers are called, Sadie?'

'No, Mummy,' Sadie replied.

'They're called forget-me-nots,' Yvonne informed her.

'Oh! That's a nice name,' said Sadie.

After about twenty minutes in the play area, they made their way back, passing by the same flowerbed. 'Do you remember what these pretty flowers are called, Sadie?' said Yvonne.

'Of course I do!' she replied, 'They're called "don't forgets".'

John Lawton

'I want a haircut please.'
'Certainly, which one?'

Oliver Marshall

Patient: Doctor, doctor. I snore so loudly that I keep myself awake.
Doctor: Well, sleep in another room then.

David Shaw

A seven-year-old girl told her mother that a little boy in her class had asked her to play doctors.

'Oh dear, what happened?' the girl's mum asked worriedly.

'Nothing,' replied the girl. 'He made me wait forty-five minutes, and then double-billed the insurance company.'

Rob Mellowship

When my son Tom was about three years old, we were sitting in the garden having a picnic when our cat came over to see what we were eating (as they always seem to do). We were counting flowers together, and I said that Mittens, our cat, had four legs. 'Yes, Mummy, he's got one on each corner,' came Tom's reply.

Sara Jowett

Q: Why did the cat stop?

A: He was waiting for a paws.

Cara Hodgson-Reed

Teacher: Where is your homework?

Pupil: Our furnace stopped working and we had to burn it to stop ourselves from freezing.

Ryan Jones (age seven)

A mouse was walking along a river bank in the jungle, when he spied an elephant in the water. The mouse shouted out to the elephant, 'Hey you, get out of there!'

The elephant got out of the water and asked, 'What do you want?'

'It's all right, you can get back in now,' the mouse replied, and he walked off up the river bank.

Further along, the mouse spotted a water buffalo in the river, and shouted, 'Hey you, get out of there!'

'What do you want?' said the buffalo, as he emerged from the water.

The mouse answered, 'It's all right, you can get back in now,' and walked off.

The water buffalo returned to the river, waded up to the hippo and asked him, 'Have you seen that mouse going up and

(cont.)

down the river bank telling folk to get out
of the water?'

'Yes,' said the hippo. 'What does he want?'

'I don't know,' the buffalo responded, looking
baffled. 'As soon as he asks you to get out
of the water, and you do exactly as he
says, he tells you to go back in again!'

'Well, if he demands that I get out of the
river for no good reason, I'm just going to
stamp on him!' said the hippo.

Sure enough, the mouse soon reached the
place where the hippo was bathing, and
shouted to him, 'Hey you, get out of there!'

So the hippo got out and asked the mouse
what it was he wanted. The mouse simply
said, 'It's all right, you can get back in now.'

The hippo grew very angry at this, and
called out to the mouse, 'No! You've been
telling folk to get out of the water

all day – tell me why you keep
asking or I'll stamp on you!'
The mouse looked most upset and
answered, 'I'm trying to find out who's
stolen my swimming cossie!'

Chris Horton

I came home after work one evening to find my daughter Maddy watching the usual garish cartoons. 'Right,' I said. 'Let's watch a proper programme, not this old rubbish – anyway, *Thunderbirds* is on the other side.'

Maddy looked at me very wistfully and thoughtfully, then, leaning forward to look me straight in the eye, she said, 'They're not real people, Daddy!'

Jim Reynolds

Q: Did you hear about the stupid kamikaze pilot?

A: He flew fifty-seven missions.

Roger Downs

Q: What do you call a lady with two toilets on her head?

A: Lulu.

Molly Morgan (age six)

One Sunday morning, a priest woke up and decided he was going to have a game of golf. He called his churchwarden to say that he felt sick and wouldn't be able to go to work. Way up in Heaven, St Peter saw all this, and asked God, 'Are you really going to let him get away with this?'

'No, I suppose not,' replied God.

The priest embarked on a five-hour drive to a golf course where he was certain he wouldn't encounter anyone he knew. The course was empty when he arrived, so he took his first swing, hit the ball an astonishing 495 yards, and got a hole in one. St Peter watched in disbelief, and asked God, 'Why did you let him do that?'

God replied, 'Who's he going to tell?'

Rob Mellowship

Q: What happened at the cannibals' wedding party?

A: They toasted the bride and groom.

Jack Fellows

Q: What is a crocodile's favourite game?

A: Snap.

Adam Deans (age six)

My wife's nephew George was being given some spelling practice by his mother Bridget. He read, 'The cat's bowl was on the floor,' and his mother then asked him to spell 'cat's'. George spelled it aloud as C-A-T-S. His mother said, 'That was very good, George, but it is C-A-T-apostrophe-S.'

The next day, George was reading to his mother again. When he got to the passage about the cat's bowl, he spelt it out loud as C-A-T, but then paused to think, and said, 'Catastrophe-S!'

David Wragg

Some years ago I had my three best friends visiting for the day, and one had brought along her sons Robert, aged three, and Edward, who was nearly two. After lunch it was time for young Robert to use the 'facilities'. In a very grown-up manner he asked me to show him the way, and I did. He went in by himself and shut the door. Almost immediately, we heard his voice ring out reassuringly, 'It's all right, Mummy, it's a clean one – it's got Bloo in it!'

Linda Weeks

Q: What do vampires have at eleven o'clock every day?

A: A coffin break.

Ruth Jarvis

Q: What does a cat get when he's ill?

A: Cat~arrh.

Cara Hodgson-Reed

Q: How do you know if an elephant has been in your fridge?

A: By the footprints in the butter.

Debi Beeson

On arriving at our rented holiday villa in Spain, our grandson Evan, aged five, rushed down to the pool and threw a ball on the calm surface of the water, as boys do. On seeing the ripples spreading over the surface, he shouted excitedly, 'Look at the wrinkles on the pool!'

Catriona Thomson

Q: What is the longest word in the dictionary?

A: The word 'smiles', because there's a mile between each 'S'.

Ann Hodgson

'Knock, knock.'
'Who's there?'
'Isabel.'
'Isabel who?'
'Isabel necessary on a bike?'

Ken Cook

Q: Which part of a fish weighs the most?

A: Its scales.

Dan Parker (age eight)

Q: Did you hear about the hyena who swallowed an Oxo cube?

A: He made a laughing stock of himself.

Celia Buckley

About twenty years ago we lived in a small council flat in East London, and our son Mark would often ask why we couldn't live in a house with a garden. We told him that, unfortunately, Mummy and Daddy couldn't afford a house. When we eventually managed a council transfer to a house with a garden in Eltham, Mark asked how we got it, and we told him the council had given it to us.

A few weeks later, Mark, being a Ferrari fan, asked if he could have a red Ferrari. We told him we couldn't afford it, so he said, 'Can't you get one from the council?'

Mary and Michael Watson

Q: What do you call a pig with
no clothes on?

A: Streaky bacon.

Gemma Evans

Q: What did the policeman say to his
belly button?

A: You're under a vest.

Ruby Schofield (age nine) and Lisa Wooster

Teacher: Who can tell me where
Hadrian's Wall is?
Pupil: I expect it's around
Hadrian's garden, Miss.

Abby Gardener

Teacher: It's time for your violin lesson.
Pupil: Oh, fiddle.

Jean Bowers

Q: Why do idiots eat biscuits?
A: Because they're crackers.

Jane Carter

Q: How does a frog with a broken leg feel?
A: Very unhoppy.

Jill McDermott

Our granddaughter Rebekah was once staying the night with her other grandma. At bedtime Rebekah's pyjamas could not be found, and, after looking everywhere in desperation, Grandma asked Rebekah, 'What do they look like?'

Rebekah replied sagely, 'Looks like they're lost, Grandma.'

Roger Long

A rabbit went into a butcher's shop and asked for a lettuce. The butcher said, 'We sell meat, not vegetables – I'll give you one out of my garden, but don't come back again.'

The following day the rabbit came back and asked for another lettuce. The butcher went mad and said, 'I'm not a greengrocer – we sell meat!' But once again he gave the rabbit a lettuce from his garden, and said, 'If you come back again, I'll fasten your ears to the floor with five-inch nails.'

The next day the rabbit returned once again, and this time he asked for a pound of five-inch nails. When the butcher replied that he didn't have any, the rabbit said, 'Right then, I'll have a lettuce instead!'

Lew Speight

Q: What do demons have on holiday?

A: A devil of a time.

Amy Dewson (age six)

One fat cat said to a slim cat,
'How do you stay so slim?'
The slim cat replied, 'I'm on the
catkins diet.'

Cara Hodgson-Reed

A long time ago, a little girl of our acquaintance came home from school one afternoon, highly delighted with herself, having learned to say a new prayer: 'Our Father, who walked into Heaven, "Hello, what's your name?"' The Alternative Lord's Prayer, perhaps?

Clare Fletcher

A couple were due to have their baby christened in the parish church. Before the ceremony, the mother had decided to prime the godfather about the baby's name, knowing that he and the baby's father would be in the local pub immediately before the service, raising a few toasts to the baby, and he would therefore be liable to forget anything he was told afterwards.

The ceremony was going well until the priest asked the godparents, 'What name do we give this child?' Due to the effects of the earlier drinking session, the godfather replied, 'Spindonna.'

The priest continued, 'I name this child Spindonna,' to which the mother cried out, 'No, it's not Spindonna — I said, "The name is pinned on her dress."'

Stanley Hope

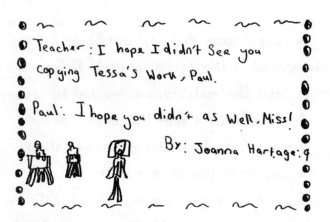

Teacher: I hope I didn't see you copying Tessa's work, Paul.

Paul: I hope you didn't as well, Miss!

By: Joanna Hartage.

Looking around one of our wonderful National Trust houses one day, my mother, daughter and I came across a rather ornate, horse-drawn hearse in one of the stables. I must admit it was a sight to behold, as it was beautifully restored and the engraved glass panels were breathtaking. My five-year-old daughter Heather stood there, holding her grandma's hand, mesmerized. After a short silence, Heather said, 'Oh Grandma, I bet whoever had to ride in that really enjoyed themselves.'

Grandma, trying to stifle a little giggle, replied, 'I expect they did, darling.'

Marcia Kempston

Q: How did the Vikings send secret messages?

A: By Norse code.

Paul Jackson

Q: Which fish do road menders use?

A: Pneumatic krill.

Katie Harper

Q: Why did the witch wear a green felt pointy hat?

A: So she could walk across snooker tables without being seen.

Matthew Innes (age seven)

I had been out shopping one day and returned home with my children; Ann was just a few months old and her brother Tony was two. There was a step up to the front door of our bungalow, and I often found it quite difficult to get the pram inside. I lifted Tony out of the pram and opened the front door. However, while I was turning the pram round to get it indoors, Tony went inside and closed the door behind him. When I looked through the front-room window, he was sitting smugly in the armchair grinning at me. He was a tall two-year-old and, after a few minutes, he decided he was going to let me in. After that little episode, I always made sure I had the back-door key with me as well as the key for the front door.

Janice Clough

First kid: My mum took me to the optician's yesterday, and guess who I bumped into?
Second kid: Everybody.
Bruce Biddie

Q: How do snails get their shells so shiny?
A: They use snail varnish.
Debbie Reed

Pupil 1: I failed every subject except for algebra.

Pupil 2: How did you keep from failing that?

Pupil 1: I didn't take algebra.

Hugh Frampton

Q: What's a vampire's favourite sport?

A: Batminton.

Helen Newson

Q: Why was the Egyptian girl worried?

A: Because her daddy was a mummy.

Frances Lipsey

When my nephew Stephen was three, he came to my niece Caroline's christening. The vicar went to the lectern, which had a large, carved, wooden eagle on it, to give the sermon. Stephen, who had been sitting very quietly listening to him, suddenly turned to me and said in a loud voice, 'Why is he talking to that parrot?' We were all in hysterics for the rest of the service.

Judith Mewies

Q: Which prehistoric monster wrote novels?

A: Bronte~saurus.

Bob Reeve

Q: What is the definition of a tornado?

A: Mother Nature doing the twist.

Karen Spires

Q: What do you get if you cross a cow with a chicken?

A: Cock-a-doodle-moo.

Emily Bowden (age eight)

Patient: Doctor, doctor. My little boy has just swallowed a roll of film.

Doctor: Hmmmm. Let's hope nothing develops.

Edward Hope (age seven)

Q: How do you start a jelly race?

A: Get set.

Adam Deans (age six)

Q: What do you get if you cross an elephant with a Boy Scout?

A: An elephant that helps little old ladies across the road.

Frank Holmes

One day when my daughter was five and had just started school, I asked her what she'd done that day. 'We learned what keeps everything on the ground,' she replied.

'Oh yes,' I said, 'and what is it?'

'Grabbity,' she said with a big smile. 'It stops everything from floating away 'cos it grabs everything on to the floor.'

Kevin Haith

Q: What do you get if you cross a big fish with an electricity pylon?

A: An electric shark.

Stewart Riley

Q: How do you get five donkeys in an ambulance?

A: Two in the front, two in the back, and one on the roof going, 'Eeeor eeeor eeeor.'

Thomas Cammidge (age six)

Q: How many balls of string would it take to reach the moon?

A: Just one, if it's long enough.

Wendy Stone

Q: Why did the knight run around shouting for a tin opener?

A: He had a bee in his suit of armour.

Rebecca Horner

Q: What's a cat's favourite colour?

A: Purrrrrrr...ple.

Stephen Ackroyd

Q: What does Tarzan sing at Christmas?

A: 'Jungle Bells.'

David Humphreys (age eight)

A man went to the doctor and said, 'Doctor, doctor, I've had a strawberry on my head for two days.'
The doctor replied, 'Oh, that's no good — you need some cream on that.'

Andrew Lane

What do you call a girl with a sausage on her head?

A BARBIE!

Timothy Andrew Richardson 6B Age. 10

Q: What sort of pet makes the loudest noise?

A: A trum~pet.

Amanda Barker

Q: What do you give a pony with a cold?

A: Cough stirrup.

Marianne Taylor

Q: Why can't a car play football?

A: Because it's only got one boot.

Andy Smith

Q: What is the definition of a slug?

A: A snail with a housing problem.

Dennis Porter

A man walked into a fish~and~chip shop with a fish under his arm. 'Do you sell fish cakes?' he asked the assistant.

'Yes, we do,' came the reply.

'Thank goodness for that,' said the man. 'It's his birthday today.'

Sue Newman and James Hinchliffe

Q: What did the chick say when its mum laid an orange?

A: Oh, look what marmalade.

Colin and Jane Hartridge

Q: What do you call a snowman with a suntan?

A: A puddle.

Vicki Simms

Q: What is yellow and pinches your bath soap?

A: A robber duck.

Andrea Pleant

Q: What is the difference between illegal and unlawful?

A: Unlawful is breaking the law, and illegal is a sick bird.

Dave and Tina

When our son Adrian was eight and his sister Fiona (who had very dark brown eyes) was two, he looked at her and said, 'Fiona, when you look out of your eyes, do you see chocolate buttons?'

Jean McDonald Scott

Q: Why did the lettuce get embarrassed?

A: Because he saw the salad dressing.

Andy Sindle

Q: Why does Superman wear such big shoes?

A: Because of his amazing feats.

Frank Everett

We were out in the garden one day when my granddaughter was three or four years old, and there was a small aeroplane flying overhead. Drawing her attention to it, I decided to give the plane a name, and said, 'Look, there's Arthur the aeroplane.'

She looked up, then, in a puzzled voice, asked, 'Where's the other half, Granny?'

It took me a couple of seconds to realize what she meant!

Yvonne Stearson

Q: What is the fruitiest lesson?

A: History, because it's full of dates.

Jean Weeks

Q: How many skunks does it take to make a big stink?

A: A phew.

Amy (age six) and Matthew (age three)

While we were eating supper recently, I was trying to express an interest in the day of my two sons, Charlie (nine) and Edward (seven). I asked Charlie which lessons he had had that day and he told me he had done maths, which is his favourite subject. 'What did you do in maths, then?' I asked.

'We started doing something called ratios,' he replied.

Edward piped up, 'Is that Ratio Nelson?'

Lucy Whitworth

A sausage and an egg were sitting in a frying pan. The egg says to the sausage, 'It's hot in here, isn't it?' The sausage says, 'Blimey, a talking egg!'

Jacob Sheath (age five)

Q: Why is the sand wet?
A: Because the sea weed.

Flora Symons (age seven)

Q: What do you get if you cross a sheep with a kangaroo?
A: A woolly jumper.

Shannon White (age four)

The National Society for the Prevention of Cruelty to Children (NSPCC) is delighted that *Thomas's Joke Book* is supporting us to raise money for children who need our help. Our vision is of a society where all children are loved, valued and able to fulfil their potential. We work in difficult situations; helping children and their families overcome the devastating effects of cruelty, abuse and neglect.

We run 180 projects for children, young people and families who need us, and received more than 11,000 requests for help last year alone. None of our activities to end cruelty to children would be possible without the public's generosity and support. Children continue to need our help and we continue to need yours.

You can help end cruelty FULL STOP by making a donation on **020 7825 2505** or by visiting **www.nspcc.org.uk/donate**.

Thank you for your support.

NSPCC Registered charity number 216401.